DEATH BY FIELD TRIP

1 G
2 ?
3 Lilly
4 Luana
5 Jim
6 Emma
7 Sarah
8 exploration of spec...
9 flu visitor
10 the red
11 Sandstorm

Other FoxTrot Books by Bill Amend

FoxTrot
Pass the Loot
Black Bart Says Draw
Eight Yards, Down and Out
Bury My Heart at Fun-Fun Mountain
Say Hello to Cactus Flats
May the Force Be with Us, Please
Take Us to Your Mall
The Return of the Lone Iguana
At Least This Place Sells T-shirts
Come Closer, Roger, There's a Mosquito on Your Nose
Welcome to Jasorassic Park
I'm Flying, Jack . . . I Mean, Roger
Think iFruity

Anthologies

FoxTrot: The Works
FoxTrot *en masse*
Enormously FoxTrot
Wildly FoxTrot
FoxTrot Beyond a Doubt
Camp FoxTrot
Assorted FoxTrot

DEATH BY FIELD TRIP

A FoxTrot Collection by Bill Amend

**Andrews McMeel
Publishing**

Kansas City

FoxTrot is distributed internationally by Universal Press Syndicate.

01 02 03 04 05 BAH 10 9 8 7 6 5 4 3 2 1

ISBN: 0-7407-1391-4

Library of Congress Catalog Card Number: 00-108455

8

Jason the great   Jason the super-great

Jason the wonderful

Jason the amazing   Jason the great and amazing

Jason the super-wonderful, super-great and super-amazing

14

16

18

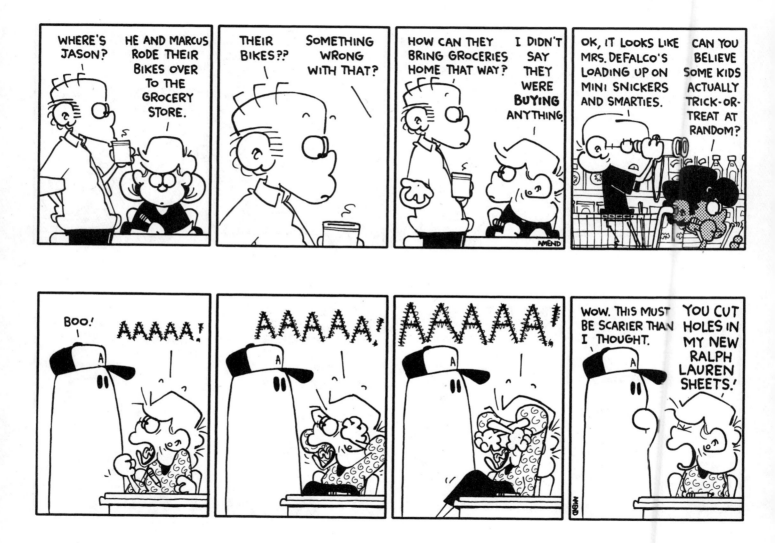

23

24

25

29

30

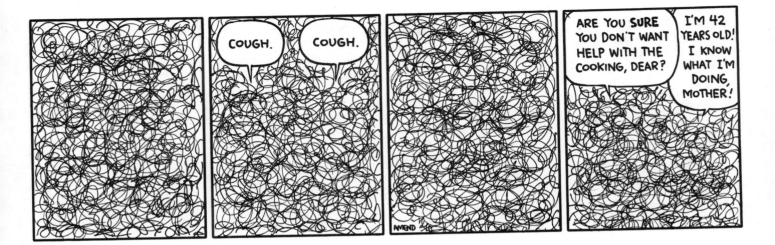

38

43

44

54

From Kidville came cries! How the tears filled their eyes!

Handkerchief set

Toothpaste

Binder paper

The screams and the sobs took Mrs. Grinch by surprise!

But those presents were USE-FUL!

"Make these kids stop! Make their whines go away!"

WAAA! BOO! WAAA! BOO!

It's said that her eardrums swelled three sizes that day!

OK! OK! You win!

Yes, old Mrs. Grinch learned a lesson to share: that Christmas doesn't come in gifts of underwear.

It comes in BIG presents that cost lots of dough! It comes in BIG boxes! It comes with a bow!

Cash! That's good, too!

For Mrs. Grinch saw, when it comes time to feast, the children you love deserve the roast beast.

I SEE YOU ADDED THAT LAST PANEL SINCE I PUT DINNER IN THE OVEN.

EGGPLANT?! ON CHRISTMAS?! MOM, PLEASE!

58

60

63

66

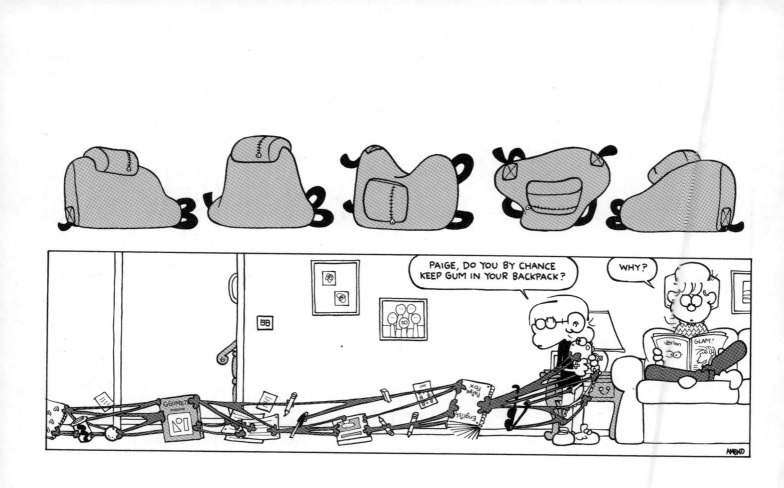

CHECKMATE. CHECKMATE. CHECKMATE. CHECKMATE. CHECKMATE.
CHECKMATE. CHECKMATE. CHECKMATE. CHECKMATE. CHECKMATE.
IATE. CHECKMATE. CHECKM
MATE. CHECKMATE. CHECK
ATE. CHECKMATE. CHECKMA
HECKMATE. CHECKMATE. C
COMPUTERS ARE GETTING A TAD **TOO** FAST, IF YOU ASK ME.
THAT CONCLUDES OUR NEXT 250,000 MATCHES. SHALL I CONTINUE?
AMEND

JASON, I TOLD YOU TO STAY AWAY FROM ME!
AND I AM.
FoxMactor
VÖG
WHAT ARE YOU TALKING ABOUT?!
THIS IS BUT A HOLO-GRAPHIC PROJECTION OF ME. THE REAL ME IS NOWHERE NEAR YOU. SEE FOR YOUR-SELF... YOU CAN PASS YOUR HAND RIGHT THROUGH ME.
WHAP!
HA!
AMEND
PAIGE, I TOLD YOU — HIT YOUR BROTHER ONE MORE TIME AND YOU'RE GROUNDED.
BUT... BUT... MOM!
HA HA!

71

72

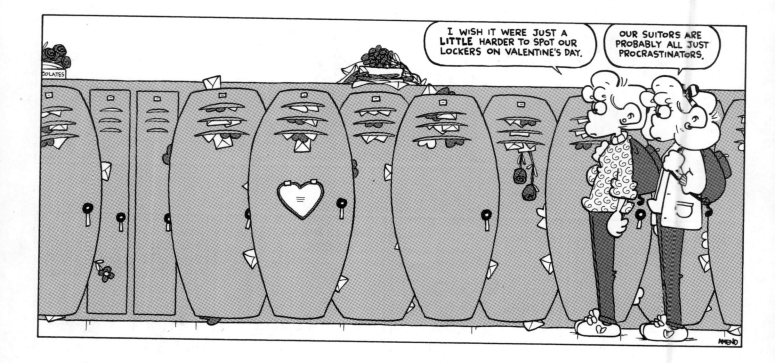

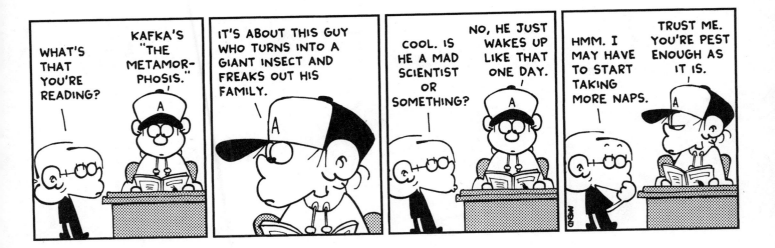

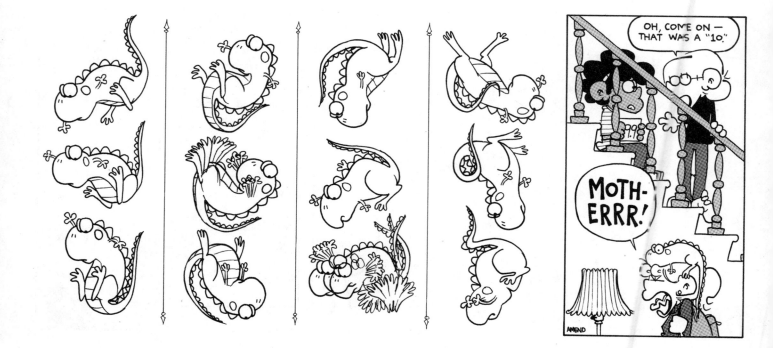

88

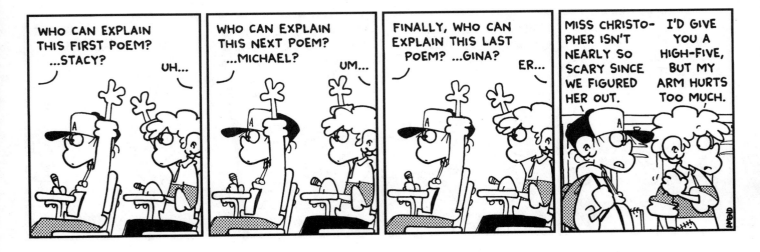

94

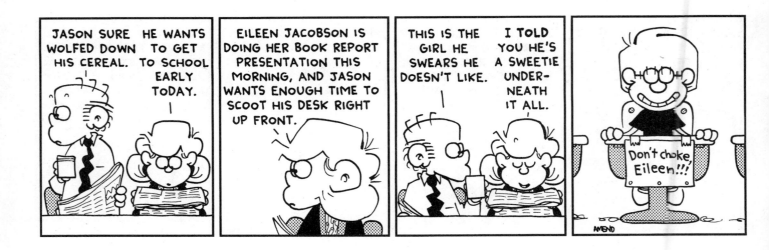

107

ACTION! I HAD A FUNNY DREAM AN HOUR OR TWO BEFORE WE STOPPED, MR. FRODO. OR MAYBE IT WASN'T A DREAM. FUNNY IT WAS ANYWAY.

WELL, WHAT WAS IT? I HAVEN'T SEEN OR THOUGHT OF ANYTHING TO MAKE ME SMILE SINCE WE LEFT LOTHLORIEN.

CUT! WHAT ARE YOU TWO DOING?! THOSE LINES AREN'T IN THE SCRIPT!

THEY'RE IN THE BOOK.

WE HAVE IT MEMORIZED.

SOMEBODY GET ME CASTING ON THE PHONE.

COULDN'T YOU THANK THEM LATER? THIS ROPE SHOULD BE MADE OF ELVEN HITHLAIN, BY THE WAY.

MORDORRR...

COOL! A RINGWRAITH!

DOOM! DOOM! DOOM!

COOL! AN ARMY OF ORCS!

GREETINGS, FRIENDS, I AM THE LADY GALADRIEL.

AAAAA! A GIRL CALLED US "FRIENDS"!

I'M PRETTY SURE WE CAN SWITCH SOME OF THAT AROUND IN EDITING.

RUN, SAM, RUN!

LOOK OUT FOR THE GAFFER, MR. FRODO, SIR!

114

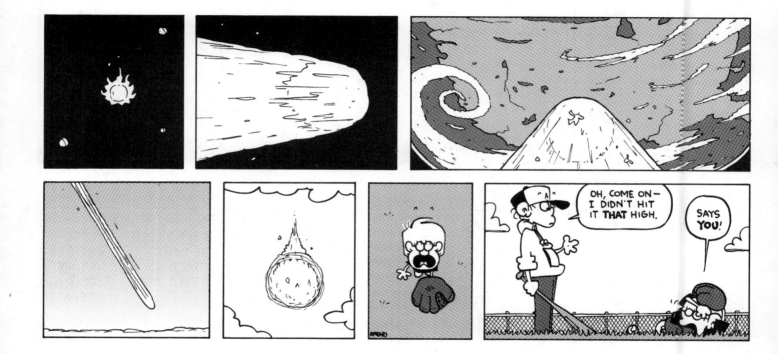